CARL LARSSON

A BOOK OF POSTCARDS

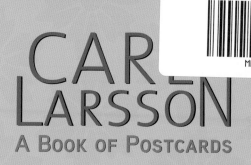

Pomegranate

PORTLAND, OREGON

Pomegranate Communications, Inc.
19018 NE Portal Way, Portland, OR 97230
800-227-1428   www.pomegranate.com

Pomegranate Europe
Number 3 Siskin Drive, Middlemarch Business Park
Coventry, CV3 4FJ, UK
+44 (0)24 7621 4461   sales@pomegranate.com

ISBN 978-0-7649-5074-2
Pomegranate Catalog No. AA598

Pomegranate publishes books of postcards on a wide range of subjects.
Please contact the publisher for more information.

Cover designed by Oky Sulistio
Printed in Korea
28 27 26 25 24 23 22 21 20 19   13 12 11 10 9 8 7 6 5 4

To facilitate detachment of the postcards from this book, fold each card along its perforation
line before tearing.

Carl Larsson (Swedish, 1853–1919)
Letter Writing, 1912
Watercolor, 52.5 x 74 cm (20^{11}/$_{16}$ x 29^{1}/$_{8}$ in.)

800 227 1428 WWW.POMEGRANATE.COM

Pomegranate

Carl Larsson (Swedish, 1853–1919)
Sunday Rest, 1900
Watercolor on paper, 68 x 104 cm (26¾ x 40¹⁵⁄₁₆ in.)

800 227 1428   WWW.POMEGRANATE.COM

Pomegranate

Carl Larsson (Swedish, 1853–1919)
A Day of Celebration (from the series, *A Home*), c. 1895
Watercolor, 32 x 43 cm (12⅝ x 16¹⁵⁄₁₆ in.)

Carl Larsson (Swedish, 1853–1919)
Breakfast Under the Big Birch (from the series, *A Home*), 1896
Watercolor, 32 x 43 cm (12⅝ x 16¹⁵⁄₁₆ in.)

800 227 1428 WWW.POMEGRANATE.COM

Pomegranate

Carl Larsson (Swedish, 1853–1919)
By the Cellar, 1917
Watercolor, 74 x 52.5 cm (29⅛ x 20¹¹⁄₁₆ in.)

© Nationalmuseum, Stockholm

800 227 1428 WWW.POMEGRANATE.COM

Pomegranate

Carl Larsson (Swedish, 1853–1919)
Martha Winslow as a Girl, 1896
Watercolor on paper, 59.5 x 38 cm (23⁷⁄₁₆ x 14¹⁵⁄₁₆ in.)

800.227.1428 WWW.POMEGRANATE.COM

Pomegranate

Carl Larsson (Swedish, 1853–1919)
Mama's and the Small Girls' Room
(from the series, *A Home*), 1897
Watercolor on paper, 32 x 43 cm (12⅝ x 16¹⁵⁄₁₆ in.)

800.227.1428   WWW.POMEGRANATE.COM

Pomegranate

Carl Larsson (Swedish, 1853–1919)
Daddy's Room (from the series, *A Home*), 1894–1897
Watercolor on paper, 32 x 43 cm (12⅝ x 16¹⁵⁄₁₆ in.)

800 227 1428 WWW.POMEGRANATE.COM

Pomegranate

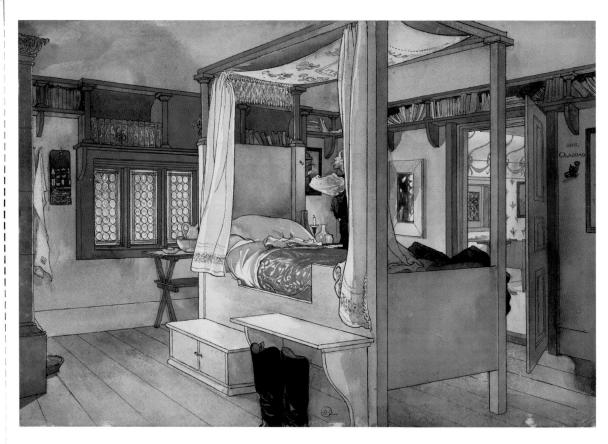

Carl Larsson (Swedish, 1853–1919)
Flowers on the Windowsill (from the series, *A Home*), 1894
Watercolor on paper, 32 x 43 cm (12⅝ x 16¹⁵⁄₁₆ in.)

800 227 1428   WWW.POMEGRANATE.COM

Pomegranate

Carl Larsson (Swedish, 1853–1919)
The Studio, the Other Half
(from the series, *A Home*), 1894–1895
Watercolor on paper, 32 x 43 cm (12⅝ x 16¹⁵⁄₁₆ in.)

800 227 1428   WWW.POMEGRANATE.COM

Pomegranate

Carl Larsson (Swedish, 1853–1919)
A Pleasant Bathing Place (from the series, *A Home*), 1896
Watercolor, 32 x 43 cm (12⅝ x 16¹⁵⁄₁₆ in.)

Carl Larsson (Swedish, 1853–1919)
In the Corner (from the series, *A Home*), c. 1895
Watercolor on paper, 32 x 43 cm (12⅝ x 16¹⁵⁄₁₆ in.)

800 227 1428 WWW.POMEGRANATE.COM

Pomegranate

Carl Larsson (Swedish, 1853–1919)
Lisbeth Reading, 1904
Watercolor, charcoal, and tempera on paper,
60 x 76 cm (23⅝ x 29¹⁵/₁₆ in.)

800 227 1428   WWW.POMEGRANATE.COM

Pomegranate

Carl Larsson (Swedish, 1853–1919)
The Studio, One Half (from the series, *A Home*), 1894–1897
Watercolor, 32 x 43 cm (12⅝ x 16¹⁵⁄₁₆ in.)

800 227 1428 WWW.POMEGRANATE.COM

Pomegranate

Carl Larsson (Swedish, 1853–1919)
The Kitchen (from the series, *A Home*), 1898
Watercolor, 32 x 43 cm (12⅜ x 16¹⁵⁄₁₆ in.)

Pomegranate

800 227 1428 WWW.POMEGRANATE.COM

Carl Larsson (Swedish, 1853–1919)
Old Anna (from the series, *A Home*), 1896
Watercolor, 32 x 43 cm (12⅝ x 16¹⁵⁄₁₆ in.)

800 227 1428 WWW.POMEGRANATE.COM

Pomegranate

Carl Larsson (Swedish, 1853–1919)
The Dining Room (from the series, *A Home*), 1894–1897
Watercolor on paper, 32 x 43 cm (12⅝ x 16¹⁵⁄₁₆ in.)

Pomegranate

800 227 1428   WWW.POMEGRANATE.COM

Carl Larsson (Swedish, 1853–1919)
Lisbeth Angling (from the series, *A Home*), 1898
Watercolor on paper, 32 x 43 cm (12⅝ x 16¹⁵⁄₁₆ in.)

800 227 1428 WWW.POMEGRANATE.COM

Pomegranate

Carl Larsson (Swedish, 1853–1919)
The Bridge (from the series, *A Home*), 1897
Watercolor, 32 x 43 cm (12⅝ x 16¹⁵⁄₁₆ in.)

Pomegranate

800 227 1428 WWW.POMEGRANATE.COM

© Nationalmuseum, Stockholm

Carl Larsson (Swedish, 1853–1919)
The Timber Chute: Winterscene
(from the series, *A Home*), 1896
Watercolor on paper, 32 x 43 cm (12⅝ x 16¹⁵/₁₆ in.)

800 227 1428 WWW.POMEGRANATE.COM

Pomegranate

Carl Larsson (Swedish, 1853–1919)
The Veranda (from the series, *A Home*), 1896–1897
Watercolor on paper, 32 x 43 cm (12⅝ x 16¹⁵⁄₁₆ in.)

Carl Larsson (Swedish, 1853–1919)
The Cottage (from the series, *A Home*), 1894–1895
Watercolor on paper, 32 x 43 cm (12⅝ x 16¹⁵⁄₁₆ in.)

Carl Larsson (Swedish, 1853–1919)
Brita's Forty Winks (from the series, *A Home*), 1894
Watercolor, 32 x 43 cm (12⅝ x 16¹⁵⁄₁₆ in.)

800 227 1428   WWW.POMEGRANATE.COM

Pomegranate

Carl Larsson (Swedish, 1853–1919)
Cozy Corner (from the series, *A Home*), c. 1894
Watercolor, 32 x 43 cm (12⅝ x 16¹⁵⁄₁₆ in.)

© Nationalmuseum, Stockholm

Carl Larsson (Swedish, 1853–1919)
When the Children Have Gone to Bed
(from the series, *A Home*), c. 1894–1897
Watercolor, 32 x 43 cm (12⅝ x 16¹⁵⁄₁₆ in.)

800 227 1428   WWW.POMEGRANATE.COM

Pomegranate

Carl Larsson (Swedish, 1853–1919)
Between Christmas and New Year (from the series, *A Home*), c. 1896
Watercolor, 32 x 43 cm (12⅝ x 16¹⁵⁄₁₆ in.)

© Nationalmuseum, Stockholm

800 227 1428   WWW.POMEGRANATE.COM

Pomegranate

Born into poverty, Carl Larsson (Swedish, 1853—1919) earned a scholarship at the Stockholm Academy of Fine Arts and supported himself as a commercial illustrator. His career in fine art, in which his ambitions tended toward the monumental and allegorical, was lackluster, but this changed when he met his future wife, artist Karin Bergöö. Under her influence he began to produce light, bright watercolors, modest in scale and subject. Karin's father gave the newlyweds a small cottage in the rural village of Sundborn, and as their family expanded, they lavished energy on remodeling and decorating their home, which became an integral part of his paintings. Larsson, whose style was a unique amalgam of Swedish folk traditions, English Arts and Crafts design ideas, and Art Nouveau and Japanese influences, is still revered as Sweden's best-loved artist.